Animal Homes

Ants and Their Nests

red carpenter ant

by Linda Tagliaferro

Consulting Editor: Gail Saunders-Smith, Ph.D.

Consultant: Gary A. Dunn, Director of Education
Young Entomologists' Society
Lansing, Michigan

Mankato, Minnesota

Pebble Plus is published by Capstone Press
151 Good Counsel Drive, P.O. Box 669, Mankato, Minnesota 56002
www.capstonepress.com

Printed in the United States of America

1 2 3 4 5 6 09 08 07 06 05 04

Library of Congress Cataloging-in-Publication Data
Tagliaferro, Linda.
Ants and their nests / by Linda Tagliaferro.
p. cm.—(Pebble Plus, Animal homes)
Summary: Simple text and photographs describe ants and the nests in which they live.
Includes bibliographical references (p. 23) and index.
ISBN 0-7368-2380-8 (hardcover)
1. Ants—Nests—Juvenile literature. [1. Ants—Nests. 2. Ants—Habits and behavior.]
I. Title. II. Series.
QL568.F7T24 2004
595.79'6—dc22 2003013421

Editorial Credits
Martha E. H. Rustad, editor; Linda Clavel, series designer; Deirdre Barton and Wanda Winch, photo researchers; Karen Risch, product planning editor

Photo Credits
Brady Clavel, 19
Bruce Coleman Inc./John Mitchell, 4–5
Corbis/Anthony Bannister, Gallo Images, 16–17; George B. Diebold, cover; Michael Rose, Frank Lane Picture Agency, 20–21
McDonald Wildlife Photography/Joe McDonald, 1
Minden Pictures/Frans Lanting, 7; Gerry Ellis, 8–9; Konrad Wothe, 10–11; Mark Moffett, 14–15
Tom Stack & Associates/Milton Rand, 13

Note to Parents and Teachers

The Animal Homes series supports national science standards related to life science. This book describes and illustrates ants and their nests. The images support early readers in understanding the text. The repetition of words and phrases helps early readers learn new words. This book also introduces early readers to subject-specific vocabulary words, which are defined in the Glossary section. Early readers may need assistance to read some words and to use the Table of Contents, Glossary, Read More, Internet Sites, and Index/Word List sections of the book.

Word Count: 150
Early-Intervention Level: 16

Table of Contents

Building Nests

Ants live in nests. Ants build their nests in the spring or fall.

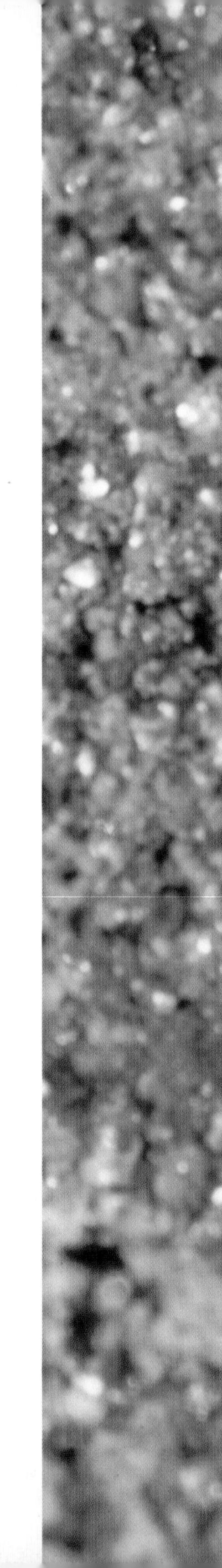

Some ants build nests
in five days. Other ants
take months to build
their nests.

Some ants build nests
with leaves and sticky silk.
Other ants build nests
in soil or wood.

tailor ants ➡

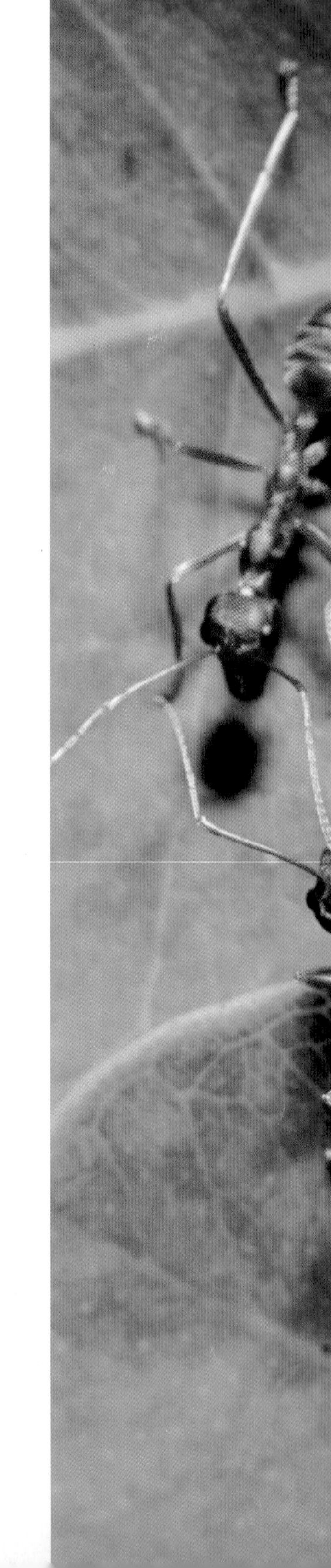

Ants dig tunnels underground or inside trees. They build chambers in the tunnels. Ants store food and raise their young in the chambers.

yellow ants ➡

Colonies and Eggs

A colony is a group of ants
living together in a nest.
Hundreds and thousands
of ants live in a colony.

red ants ➧

The queen ant lays her eggs in the nest. Worker ants take care of young ants.

fire ants ➧

Staying Safe

Some ants close the opening to their nest with pebbles. The pebbles keep out other animals.

harvester ants ➧

Some ants put twigs on top
of their nests. The twigs
keep out rain.

A Good Home

Different kinds of ants build different kinds of nests. Nests are good homes for ants.

fire ant nest ➧

Glossary

chamber—a room in an ant nest

colony—a large group of animals that live together; thousands of ants live together in some colonies.

queen ant—an adult female ant that lays eggs; most colonies have only one queen ant.

silk—a sticky fiber made by some ants

tunnel—a passage under the ground

twig—a small stick or branch

worker ant—an adult female ant that does not lay eggs; worker ants build nests and take care of young ants.

Read More

Frost, Helen. *Leaf-Cutting Ants.* Rain Forest Animals. Mankato, Minn.: Pebble Books, 2003.

Loewen, Nancy. *Tiny Workers: Ants in Your Backyard.* Backyard Bugs. Minneapolis: Picture Window Books, 2003.

Robinson, W. Wright. *How Insects Build Their Amazing Homes.* Animal Architects. Woodbridge, Conn.: Blackbirch Press, 1999.

Internet Sites

FactHound offers a safe, fun way to find Internet sites related to this book. All of the sites on FactHound have been researched by our staff.

Here's how:

1. Visit *www.facthound.com*
2. Type in this special code **0736823808** for age-appropriate sites. Or enter a search word related to this book for a more general search.
3. Click on the **Fetch It** button.

FactHound will fetch the best sites for you!

Index/Word List